Text copyright © 2008
by Harriet Ziefert Inc.
Illustrations copyright © 2008 by Yukiko Kido
All rights reserved
CIP Data is available.
Published in the United States 2008 by
 Blue Apple Books
515 Valley Street, Maplewood, NJ 07040
www.blueapplebooks.com
Distributed in the U.S. by Chronicle Books
First Edition
Printed in China

ISBN: 978-1-934706-08-4

1 3 5 7 9 10 8 6 4 2

wet pet

Illustrated by
Yukiko Kido

flip-a

WORD

Word Families

The world is full of print. Written words are everywhere. It's impossible to learn printed words by memorizing them word, by word, by word. To make learning easier, words can be grouped into families.

The words in a word family have two or more letters that are the same. We read "ate" words and "eet" words, "et" words and "am" words. If you know "am," then it's easier to learn ram, ham, and jam.

This book has words from three different word families. All the words in a family rhyme—which means you can add other words to the group by changing the first letter.

It's okay if some of the words you think of are not *real* words. If you make "kam" or "vam" or "gam," it's not wrong— as long as you know the difference between a real word and a nonsense word.

Flip each page and presto-change-o— a new word appears!

The

et

Family

W

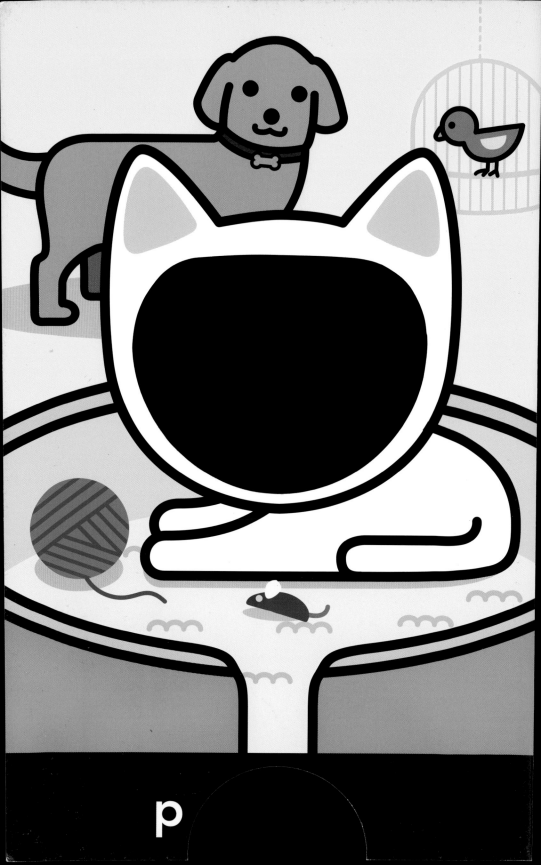

p

net

pet net

pets in a jet

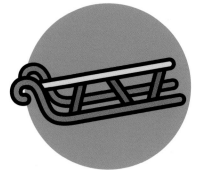

The ed Family

f
l
w
m
g
n
b
r
d
w
t

shed

b

r

sled

red sled

red bed

sled in a shed

bed sled

The

am

Family

f
l
w
m
g
n
b
r
d
w
t

jam

r

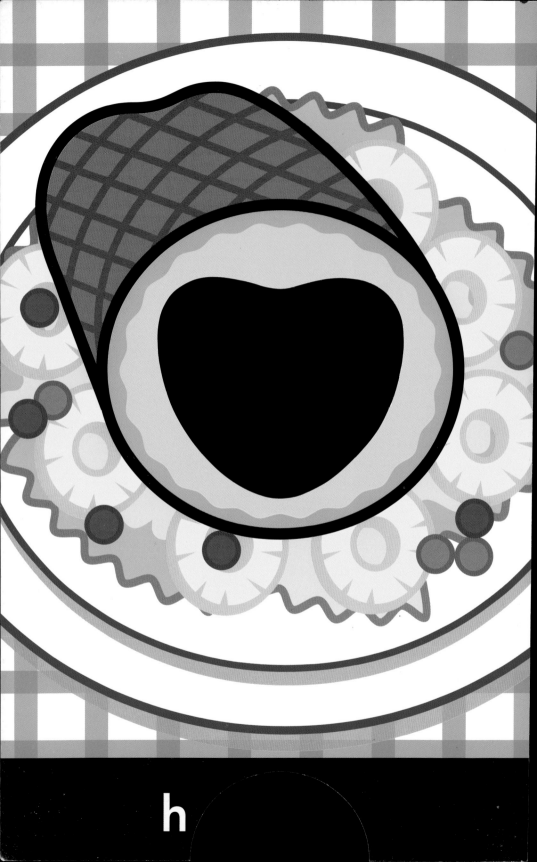

h

lamb

ram on jam

jam on lamb

ram with ham

ram and lamb with jam

The et Family

get	net
jet	pet
let	set
met	wet

The ed Family

bed	red
fed	shed
led	sled

The am Family

clam	lamb
cram	ram
ham	slam
jam	yam

Find the words in each family.

sled jet jam pet led

net get fed slam

shed lamb set

jam let clam ram

cram met pet let

yam fed ham bed

red led ram shed

net

get wet lamb jam

clam ham set red

jet sled wet

bed met

More books in the flip-a-word series from Blue Apple 🍎